Bacon

and

The Dissociation Of Sensibility

- A Reunion -

By

David Conduct

Copyright © 2022 David Conduct

All rights reserved, including the right to reproduce this book, or portions thereof in any form. No part of this text may be reproduced, transmitted, downloaded, decompiled, reverse engineered, or stored, in any form or introduced into any information storage and retrieval system, in any form or by any means, whether electronic or mechanical without the express written permission of the author.

ISBN: 9781916981911

Also by this Author

*The Great War - Lost and Found

*All you Need is Love - A Julian of Norwich Handbook

*Rock 'n' Roll Years - Journal reflection's 1973 – 1998

*Essays on a Liberal Education

*The Holy Contour of Life - A Spiritual Journey

*A Word to Planet Earth

*Kindness and the Individual - An Introduction to Vasily Grossman's "Life and Fate"
*Mending a Broken Universe

*A Gardener for Man - An Introduction to William Langland's
"Vision of Piers Plowman" (Lulu)

*Dramatis Personae - A Book of Names

*A Simpler Path via Julian of Norwich and Marcus Aurelius

*The Anatomy of Melancholy - An abridged version of Robert Burton's book

All titles, except "A Gardener for Man" available from Amazon

Bibliography

K. Armstrong *The Battle for God*

Francis Bacon *The Advancement of Learning*
Novum Organum (from Instauratio Magna)

J. Bronowski *The Ascent of Man*

E. A. Burtt *The Metaphysical Foundations of Modern Science*

R. G. Collingwood *The Idea of Nature*

D. Conduct *All You Need is Love*
Essays on a Liberal Education
Mending a Broken Universe

T. S. Eliot *The Metaphysical Poets*

P. S. Freund *Myths of Creation*

J. Lovelock *Gaia - A New Look at Planet Earth*

L. C. Knights *Explorations*

G. Tonnelli *Cosmos*

J. West *The Great Intellectual Revolution*

A. Woolf *A History of Science, Technology and Philosophy*
Sixteenth and Seventeenth Centuries

K. Armstrong *Sacred Nature*

For Peter Coveney

Hull University

1960 – 61

And

John Hale

Warwick University

1967 – 68

The Title-Page of Bacon's *Novum Organum*

CONTENTS

PREFACE 1
INTRODUCTION 3
THE ARISTOTELIAN BACKGROUND 4
BACON'S CHALLENGE TO ARISTOTLE 8
L. C. KNIGHTS EVALUATION OF BACON 13
WHAT WE HAVE LOST 18
A REUNION OF THOUGHT AND FEELING 23
E. A. BURTT'S EVALUATION 33
MIND OVER MATTER 38
Benevolence 40
Native American Wisdom 41
POSTSCRIPT 42

PREFACE

I first became aware of the term "dissociation of sensibility" in the context of research into the Scientific Revolution of the Seventeenth Century, under the guidance of Peter Coveney, my Renaissance tutor at Hull University 1960 – 61.

Subsequently, of course, I learned that the term had no scientific origins and that it arose from an essay by T. S. Eliot on *The Metaphysical Poets* (1921). In this essay Eliot had tried to defend these poets from Samuel Johnson's criticism of them by observing that they were the direct heirs of an earlier age and, like their Elizabethan predecessors, were intellectual poets who 'felt' their thoughts and possessed "a mechanism of sensibility which could devour any experience." Eliot claimed that in the Seventeenth Century "a dissociation of sensibility set in, from which we have never recovered," and through which poetic expression had become radically changed.

Eliot linked this dissociation with the work of Milton and Dryden and later, in another essay, Milton II ,to events taking place in the English Civil War, 1642 – 49. In fact, however, the term has its true origin in the development of Scientific thought in the Seventeenth Century rather than in the realms of poesy and its significance goes far beyond mere literary expression.

In my studies of the Scientific Revolution I found support for this view in an essay by L. C. Knights on "Bacon and the Seventeenth Century Dissociation of Sensibility," in his *Explorations* published in 1946. In this, Knights identifies Francis Bacon (1561 – 1626) as the principal source of a new mode of thought which would, in time, challenge and replace almost entirely the cultural heritage of Aristotle which had shaped the thinking of Western Europe for over 2000 years. In the process, Bacon came to separate thought from feeling and a dissociation of sensibility set in which would change not simply poetic expression but our whole way of thinking and our entire relationship with the natural world.

INTRODUCTION

Knights sees Bacon as the prophet of modern, scientific rationalism, and his aim was the acquisition of new knowledge through inductive reasoning and the improvement of human life by means of it. These are the driving thoughts behind his two major works, *The Advancement of Learning*, published in 1605 and *Novum Organum* in 1620.

According to Knights, Bacon is essentially a theoretician. He was not himself an experimental scientist, like Galileo, and he had no involvement in, nor awareness of the mathematical physics which was to shape the Scientific Revolution of the Seventeenth Century. His fundamental importance, therefore, lies in the realm of ideas and his advocacy of the scientific method.

The intellectual background to Bacon was shaped by Aristotelian scholasticism, classical humanism, and occultism. While he had some sympathy for the natural magic espoused by occultists, such as John Dee, and some respect for the literary achievements of classical humanists, Bacon had no time at all for the Aristotelian framework of knowledge which still dominated European thought and was based upon deductive reasoning – the logical progression from first principles to established truths. Bacon's whole intellectual career was essentially a crusade against this mode of thought.

THE ARISTOTELIAN BACKGROUND

For Dante, and many others, Aristotle (384-322 B.C.) was always "the master of those who know." His lecture notes on a vast range of subjects including logic, rhetoric, poetics, physics, biology, psychology, mathematics, ethics and politics survived to shape the culture of Western Europe for over 2000 years.

In Aristotle, rational argument in the form of deductive logic was combined with natural philosophy based on observation (Aristotle's first love was always biology) to create a cosmology ultimately founded upon philosophical rather than scientific truths.

By the Thirteenth Century, the rediscovery of Aristotle's lost works on Logic and Natural Philosophy, largely via translations from Arabic versions of his texts, had generated a ferment of intellectual activity in Western Europe and led directly to the foundation of the first universities. To a Europe still recovering from the collapse of the Roman Empire and the ensuing Dark Ages, Aristotle's work was a revelation and it came to form the core of university studies.

From the Thirteenth to the Sixteenth Century the Arts Course at Paris consisted of Grammar, Rhetoric, and Philosophy, beginning with Logic and ending with Physics. Grammar was generally studied between the ages of ten and twelve; Rhetoric from twelve to fourteen. Philosophy was begun at the age of fifteen and its course in Logic, Metaphysics, Moral Philosophy and Natural Science was completed by about the age of twenty.

Mastery of Aristotle's Logic became all-important in the student's course of studies but unfortunately, failing to develop adequate symbolism, the language of Logic became highly technical and specialised. Consider, for example, one of the basic rules which a medieval student of fifteen or sixteen was expected to master:

"The second rule is that a proposition concerning the infinite, taken syncategorematically, is expounded by a copulative whose first part affirms the predicate of the subject taken according to some quantity, continuous or discrete, and whose second part denies that the predicate is in such a subject according to a determined quantity…" (W. Ong *Ramus, Method and the Decay of Dialogue* 75)

This domination of Aristotle's Logic was bitterly resented by classical humanists in the Sixteenth Century, looking for more elegant forms of expression. Bacon shared their misgivings but his opposition to Aristotle focussed more upon his concerns regarding the efficacy of "logic chopping" and deductive reasoning in the pursuit of truth, and the erroneous theories regarding the natural world which resulted from this way of thinking.

The Universe as conceived by Aristotle and later embodied in Ptolemy's *Almagest*, was a harmonious, finite whole of which the Earth was the fixed centre. Around the earth moved the heavens in a series of concentric, crystal spheres whose fountain-head was the sphere of the Primum Mobile, or First Mover, whose divine harmony caused the circular motion of the whole celestial system.

The material, sub-lunar world of human existence was composed of the four elements: earth, air, fire and water. Various mixtures of the elements were made to represent every kind of matter known to man, and the behaviour of the physical world was explained by the constant attempts of the elements to return to their proper stations in the sub-lunary sphere. Fire, for example, was the lightest element and so its natural place was believed to be in an invisible belt high above the surface of the Earth, where occasionally comets and meteors were formed from its substance.

Movement within this Universe was explained by Aristotle in terms of two kinds of motion – natural and unnatural. Natural motion was the disposition of a body towards certain kinds of movement. Thus, the natural motion of fire and air was upwards, that of earth and water downwards. In contrast to the rectilinear direction of the elements, the natural movement of the celestial spheres was circular, as befitted the region of the incorruptible heavens which experienced neither decay or change. Unnatural motion, on the other hand, was violent motion since it contradicted the ordinary tendency of a body to move to what was its natural place.

Aristotle's concept of motion made the Universe a spiritual world of moving forces and this may help to explain its appeal to the Christian Middle Ages. As H. Butterfield observes, "A Universe constructed upon the mechanics of Aristotle had the door half-way open for spirits already; it was a Universe in which unseen hands had to be in constant operation and sublime intelligences had to roll the planetary spheres around. Alternatively, bodies had to be endowed with souls and aspirations, with a "disposition" to certain kinds of motion, so that matter itself seemed to possess mystical qualities." (*The Origins of Modern Science H. Butterfield*)

To a slowly-awakening civilisation such as that of Western Europe in the early Middle Ages (post-1100), a ready-made philosophy and interpretation of the Universe was highly acceptable. Unfortunately, the basis of Aristotelian cosmology was philosophical rather than scientific and derived without the medium of scientific observation and experiment. Moreover, after a long period of time, through the process of what Butterfield calls "literary transmission",its theories had become largely book-bound and out of step with reality. For Bacon, the challenge was to put this right.

BACON'S CHALLENGE TO ARISTOTLE

Bacon's studies at Cambridge University had left him disillusioned with traditional learning associated with Aristotle and, in fact, after just three years 1573-75, he gave up these studies. Henceforth, he would devote his life to the formulation of an alternative culture to that derived from Ancient Greece.

This alternative culture would be based on science and technology and would specifically aim at the general improvement of the human condition. Bacon was perfectly aware that the realisation of his programme of reform would involve a break with tradition. It would require an historical examination of the past and the result would be a change not only in man's thinking but also in his way of living; a change in his whole attitude towards the natural world and cultural tradition.

Bacon's historical attitude was profoundly influenced by the technical progress being made in the Sixteenth Century and earlier, as reflected, for example, in the printing press and the compass. In his view, such developments had radically altered the course of history and they called in question the whole authority of a traditional culture, shaped by liberal arts and sciences which retained their distaste for practical application and showed no interest in the progress of the material world.

In contrast, Bacon observed:

"In the mechanical arts, which are founded on Nature and the light of experience, we see the contrary happening, for these are continually thriving and growing, as if the breath of life inspired them." (*Novum Organum*)

If it was true, asked Bacon, that the Greeks and Romans had never invented anything that could be compared to the printing press, why should their knowledge be held in such esteem? For too long, he argued, the progress of man had been obstructed by excessive respect for the authority of the ancients. Indeed such respect was quite misplaced, for as far as the history of civilisation was concerned the ancients were really children. As he observed: "The old age of the world (i.e. the present) is to be accounted the true antiquity; and this is the attribute of our own times, not of that earlier age of the world in which the ancients lived."

Alongside Bacon's plea for a new historical perspective, went his call for a completely new approach to learning. He felt that the type of learning which had developed in the ancient world disregarded utility and emphasised, instead, the superiority of thought over action and man's resignation to Nature rather than mastery of it. Such learning was essentially literary in character and depended heavily upon the study of words rather than of things.

As an alternative to this form of culture Bacon's *Novum Organum* urged men to seek the Truth through direct observation of Nature instead of simply reading established texts. True knowledge, he claimed, could only come from things not words, since words either represent things which do not exist in Nature or else convey a very confused idea of things. Words were but the images of matter and could not be relied upon to provide a true or accurate picture of the material world. Moreover, defects in language mirrored defects in mental attitudes, arising from the human desire to see more order in the world than actually existed. As Bacon observed:

"*The human understanding is, of its own nature, prone to suppose the existence of more order and regularity in the world than it finds. And though there may be many things in Nature which are singular and unmatched, yet it devises for them conjugates and parallels and relatives, which do not exist. Hence, the fiction that all celestial bodies move in perfect circles.*"

According to Bacon, progress in knowledge and understanding would only begin when men got rid of their prejudices and opinions and approached the world of Nature with "minds washed clean".

The *Novum Organum* identifies as the first stage in this ascent to truth, the accumulation of knowledge through experiment and observation. This would then be followed by drawing conclusions from such experiments by means of inductive reasoning.

All this would be supported by the collective endeavours of numerous scientists, in imitation of the current practise among those engaged in technology and what Bacon called "the mechanical arts." In his book *The New Atlantis*, published in 1627, he outlined his theory of an ideal state, ruled by a governing body of scientists, organised into nine groups and working in specially-designed research laboratories.

This focus on a technological model is very significant because of its emphasis upon the progressive improvement in knowledge and its application for the common good. By basing our learning on such characteristics, Bacon fervently believed that it would be possible to create a type of culture supportive of material progress. This concern for progress and improvement was central to Bacon's whole philosophy. As he himself observed:

"The true and lawful goal of the sciences is simply this, that human life be endowed with new discoveries and powers."

Bacon's faith in inductive reasoning as the prime source of knowledge and his insistence on the application of such knowledge to man's improvement may be expressed in the simple aphorism: "Knowledge is power." Some two centuries before Marx, therefore, he may be said to have embraced the view that the importance of philosophy was not to understand the world, but to change it.

Bacon's cardinal belief, therefore, was that knowledge must be derived from observation, not from abstract reasoning and that it must be put to use for the benefit of mankind. And this is what makes Bacon so unique:

"For the first time the philosopher meets us not as a sedentary figure closeted away from the affairs of the world; not as a mere onlooker who seeks truth for its own sake, but as a being possessed by a passionate impulse to action, who places his knowledge at the service of practical ends and assigns to it as its greatest task the subjection of nature to the will of man... In this, Bacon's thought and feeling are entirely modern, and there is no vestige of medievalism left... The science which is placed at the service of humanity has as its final aim technical mastery, which now supplants artistic culture... Thus Bacon is one of the first to celebrate the coming of the technical age, and his doctrine is full of faith in future progress." (Rudolf Metz, quoted in Knights *Explorations* 95)

All this explains the fervent admiration felt for Bacon by many of his scientific contemporaries, reflected most obviously in the creation of organisations whose activities fulfilled, to some extent, Bacon's hopes for scientific co-operation. The two most famous of these were the Royal Society, founded in London in 1660, and the Academie des Sciences, in Paris in 1666.

Subsequently, rationalists such as Voltaire identified Bacon with the Enlightenment of the Eighteenth Century, while in the Nineteenth Century Macaulay acclaimed him as "the greatest of English Philosophers," the consequences of whose doctrine of Utility and Progress were evident throughout both science and society. (Knights op. cit. 95-6)

The effects of this utilitarian trajectory in Bacon's philosophy are discussed below.

L. C. KNIGHTS EVALUATION OF BACON

As befits a scholar whose expertise lies chiefly in the field of literary criticism, Knights' evaluation of Bacon's role in "the dissociation of sensibility" focusses upon his use of language; and, of course, this is perfectly justified. (L. C. Knights op. cit. 92-111)

Bacon, Knights reminds us, was no scientist. He made no experimental contribution to the progress of science in the Seventeenth Century and in fact his support of the inductive method as the key to scientific understanding left a lot to be desired. In his work, he makes little reference to the likes of Copernicus, Brahe, Kepler and Galileo, whose astronomical observations did so much to undermine the foundations of Aristotelian cosmology.

His importance, therefore, lies primarily in the realm of ideas and his articulation of them. It is perhaps significant that his great hero was Columbus and that discoveries in the terrestrial sphere were his chief source of inspiration – along with, of course, his antipathy towards Aristotelian scholarship, a legacy of his university studies at Cambridge.

Bacon, in fact, preferred to call himself, *buccinator novi temporis*, "the trumpeter of a New Age", and this is clearly reflected in the frontispiece to his major work, *Novum Organum*. This shows a ship in full sail, embarking westwards across the Atlantic, in search of new knowledge.

It is as the spokesman of this New Age that Knights approaches Bacon and in his evaluation of him the focus is very much upon his prose style.

Knights makes the point that Bacon's prose style is reflective of a change in sensibility that was taking place during the Seventeenth Century, since it aimed at masculine, plain expression, devoid of any light conceits which might divert the purpose of his prose. As an Elizabethan, however, Bacon was fully aware of the literary possibilities of the spoken word. This is reflected, for example, in his own use of metaphor to identify the four "distempers" affecting learning, in his 1605 *Advancement of Learning* and the weaknesses arising from our attachment to various "idols", in his *Novum Organum* of 1620.

Again, in expressing the desire to summarise the opinions of ancient philosophers concerning Nature, he warns against "the faggoting up together" of such opinions. A comment which might well have been applied to Robert Burton's *Anatomy of Melancholy*, published in 1621.

In the main, however, Bacon's prose favours the use of simile rather than metaphor as the medium for exploring the truth and can be seen as a direct challenge to the metaphorical complexity of Elizabethan language. This had reflected a world shaped largely by Aristotelian cosmology and by the normal processes of living. As Knights observes: "To Shakespeare and the majority of his contemporaries 'Nature' indicated a world of non-human life to which man was bound by intimate and essentially religious ties." (L. C. Knights op. cit. 102)

Bacon, however, remained emotionally detached from Nature and in this divorce of Nature and the senses can be found the true source of that "dissociation of sensibility" to which Eliot refers in his essay on *The Metaphysical Poets*.

Bacon, Knights tells us, was convinced that one of the main obstacles in the path to a true understanding of

Nature was the misuse of language. "The first distemper of learning," he writes, "is when men study words and not matter, for words are but the images of matter…and to fall in love with them is to fall in love with a picture." (Quoted by Knights op. cit. 102)

Flights of poetic fancy are therefore to be avoided in the interpretation of Nature and pride of place given to exact descriptions and rational analysis. "It is almost necessary," Bacon tells us, "in all controversies and disputations to imitate the wisdom of the Mathematicians, in setting down in the very beginning definitions of our words and terms that others may know how we accept and understand them." (Quoted L. C. Knights op. cit. 103)

Bacon clearly regarded imagination as decidedly inferior to reason when it comes to working upon 'matter' and therefore regarded poetry as pleasure or play rather than a work of duty. (105 Knights op. cit.) In this way, he gives his support to that separation of imagination and reason, of thought and feeling identified by Eliot as characteristic of poetic expression ever since the Seventeenth Century.

Plain, masculine speech, conjoined with practical action would, Bacon argues in his *Advancement of Learning*, win for learning a place in the modern state, and this, the practical application of knowledge to human affairs, is a major part of his philosophy. (106 Knights op. cit.)

In conclusion, therefore, Knights locates the origins of the "dissociation of sensibility" in Bacon's advocacy of plain speech as opposed to metaphorical imagery in the pursuit of truth. This was an essential part of his crusade to challenge the Aristotelian cosmology which had dominated Western culture for so long and replace it with a fully rational approach to Nature based on inductive reasoning.

The practical and beneficial consequences of this policy are plain to see but less obvious and certainly less easy to quantify are the cultural effects of Bacon's separation of thought and feeling. The central principles of his philosophy, according to Knights "involve an attitude towards the emotions that makes against wholeness of living." (106 Knights op. cit.) His belief in the need to use the mind as a clear and equal glass to observe and identify the truth, rather than "an enchanted glass, full of superstition," ignores completely the creative and vital forces of the mind itself as reflected, for example, in the "thought" experiments of modern theoretical physicists.

There was clearly no room for emotion in Bacon's philosophy and Knights talks of the "inadequacy and barrenness of his reflections on subjects involving intimate and personal emotions. In his "Essays", for example, we find this opinion on Love: "They do best who, if they cannot but admit love, yet make it keep quarter, and sever it wholly from their affairs and actions of life." As a result, says Knights, "the whole trend of Bacon's work is to encourage the relegation of instinctive and emotional life to a sphere separate from thought and practical activity." (Knights op. cit. 107-8)

In this way, poetry and life become separate: the one a sphere of emotional sensitivity, the other a realm of practical affairs. This division of thought and feeling Knights claims began in the Seventeenth Century and leads directly to the Utilitarianism of the Nineteenth Century, "of which we are the embarrassed heirs." (Knights op. cit. 109)

As Yeats observed of the beginning of the Nineteenth Century: "The highest faculties had faded, taking the sense of beauty with them, into some sort of vague heaven and left the lower to lumber where they best could;" leaving poetry to become more poetical, while material life "reached a peak of dehumanising ugliness." (Knights op. cit. 108)

The derogation of instinct and emotion was an entirely new feature in the development of the English language and a driving force behind what Eliot defined as a "dissociation of sensibility", which has persisted into the Twenty-first Century and which goes far beyond the narrow confines of literary expression.

As Knights observes: "By the beginning of the Eighteenth Century 'Nature' had come to mean simply the daylight world of common sense and practical effort. Man had ceased to feel the 'filial bond' binding him to all that is not human, and assumed, without question, that his part was simply to observe, to understand and to dominate the world of 'matter'. Almost as much as his explicit philosophy, Bacon's prose style is an index of the emergence of the modern world." (Knights op. cit. 102)

WHAT WE HAVE LOST

L. C. Knights identifies the frontispiece to Bacon's *Novum Organum*, which shows a ship in full sail, setting out beyond the Pillars of Hercules towards the new, uncharted lands of America, as an appropriate symbol of the "American" world of scientific progress and material well-being that much of humanity now aspires to. Much had been expected of this voyage and technical mastery has indeed achieved results "far beyond the dreams of the original projectors of the voyage." But, Knights adds, "what was also not foreseen, technical mastery has been accompanied by a spiritual impoverishment that has prevented the full realisation even of the material gains." (Knights op. cit. 109)

Writing at the mid-point of a Second World War (1943) Knights was understandably pessimistic about the consequences of Bacon's philosophy and the "spiritual impoverishment" resulting from it. If anything, these doubts have magnified as we now, in the Twenty-first Century, come to terms with the results of simply regarding Nature as a storehouse of material for mankind's consumption. Reason is clearly not the whole of experience and needs to be re-united with sensibility if our relationship with Nature is to be properly understood and developed.

In attempting to do this it might be helpful to remind ourselves of what the world was like before Bacon.

Nature then was regarded as a living organism, permeated by mind. The world of Nature was not only alive but intelligent: a rational creature with a mind of its own. Most philosophers taught and most people believed that the Universe was 'animate'. It lived and flourished as did man and was susceptible to decay and even death.

What made this Aristotelian world-picture so attractive was the extent to which it faithfully mirrored everyman's view of the world. Accustomed as we are to the truths of logic and science it is perhaps difficult for us to appreciate how deeply satisfying, both intellectually and emotionally, Aristotelian cosmology was both to scholar and layman alike. In a fundamental way this explanation of the Universe was based on common sense notions which everyone could readily acknowledge by the use of their senses as, for example, the notion of the Earth's fixity.

In such a world, man's place was clearly understood. Thus the doctrine of the four elements was paralleled by other four-fold divisions, notably the medieval theory of the humours, derived from Galen: blood was warm and moist and associated with Spring; yellow bile was warm and dry and associated with Summer; black bile was cold and dry and associated with Autumn; and phlegm was cold and moist and associated with Winter. The four seasons were, in turn, associated with the four temperaments, the sanguine, the choleric, the melancholic and the phlegmatic.

In this world-picture, man was the microcosm, or little world, which reflected the macrocosm, or big world of the Universe. And yet, man was more than just a 'reflection' of the macrocosm. Before the Seventeenth Century, people thought habitually of their world in terms of metaphors. "The world was not 'like' an animal; it was 'animate'. There was correspondence between man's body and the body of the world, man's soul and the soul of the Universe." (M. H. Nicolson *The Breaking of the Circle* 2-3) The moral order was imagined to be intimately related to the physical world at every point. Disorder in the heavens led to disorder on Earth. Thus it was perfectly acceptable for dramatists to discuss scientific themes in a metaphorical way which made them intelligible to all and part of everyone's conceptual apparatus, irrespective of the formal education they might have received.

Aristotle's whole philosophy, as understood in medieval times and later, invited the union of thought and feeling. A poet, or anyone else for that matter, did not have to pretend that a natural phenomenon had a lesson for man, he could proclaim outright that it did and no one would deny it. (J. F. West *The Great Intellectual Revolution* 110) Thus, Shakespeare, writing of the death of Henry V1 was fully entitled to regard the comet as a portent, signifying disturbances in the regions below the Moon:

"Comets, importing change of times and states
Brandish your crystal tresses in the sky
And with them scourge the bad, revolting stars
That have consented unto Henry's death."
Henry VI Act 1, Scene 1

After Edmund Halley's work on comets, however, any dramatists who spoke in these terms would be inviting ridicule, and poets were left with no supernatural effects unless used in joke only. (West op. cit. 103) The scope of poetry thus became strictly limited. With reason and emotion now made quite distinct, poetry became synonymous with the world of private fantasy. In this sense, the Scientific Revolution of the Seventeenth Century effectively destroyed the world of metaphor.

Bacon, of course, welcomed this development for central to his philosophy of putting knowledge to practical use was his disregard for the emotions and his concern to get the mind functioning clearly.

One who was less happy about this development was his contemporary, the poet John Donne (1572-1631). An Elizabethan, living on the very threshold of a scientific revolution, for Donne the most popular metaphor was still the Circle, "a circle that most people believed actually existed in the perfect sphere of the planets, in the sphere of the globe, in the round head of man. This was more than analogy, to them it was truth." (M. H. Nicolson op. cit. 7) The metaphor of the Circle also influenced historical thinking, encouraging a cyclical view of history which is the complete antithesis of modern thought with its emphasis on straight line progress and development.

Donne's poetry, dating from the end of the Sixteenth Century (1590-1601), with its fondness for allusions to map-making and geographical discoveries, can be seen as the last flowering of this metaphorical culture. By the early Seventeenth Century, however, with his growing awareness of the significance of astronomical observations by Brahe, Kepler and Galileo, Donne's faith in Aristotelian cosmology began to waver.

Symmetry, proportion and harmony were now gone and in his *Anatomy of the World – The First Anniversary*, which was published in 1611, Donne identified an existential crisis in human affairs of which we are the conscious heirs:

"*And new Philosophy calls all in doubt,*
The element of fire is quite put out;
The sun is lost, and the earth and no man's wit
Can well direct him where to look for it.
And freely men confess that this world's spent,
When in the Planets and the Firmament
They seek so many new; then see that this
Is crumbled out again to his Atomies.
'Tis all in pieces, all coherence gone;

All just supply, and all Relation."
205-214

For Donne the Circle of Perfection was gone and not only the world but the whole Universe suffered corruption. The old, animate world, of which man was a living part, as it in turn was part of a living Universe, was at an end. And, indeed, it was.

"To a greater extent than he realised, John Donne was present at the death of a world: the world of Aristotle, of Ptolemy, of St. Augustine, of Dante, and of Shakespeare. In its place was only a lesser planet, turning upon its axis, taking its orderly way among other planets, moving about the Sun that had usurped the proud centre that for centuries had been the world of man. The Circle was broken." (M. H. Nicolson op. cit. 122)

A REUNION OF THOUGHT AND FEELING

In assessing Bacon's contribution to the "dissociation of sensibility" and its practical consequences for mankind, Knights is not calling for a rejection of Bacon's philosophy of Utility and Progress. "What we need," he claims, "is not to abandon reason, but simply to recognise that reason in the last three centuries is not the whole of experience, that it has mistaken the part for the whole, and imposed arbitrary limits on its own working. Both within those limits and outside them there are still gains to be won by reason, but by a reason or intelligence, that recognises the claims of the sensibility as a whole and tries to work in harmony with it." (Knights op. cit. 111)

What follows is an attempt to explore some of the ways in which a union of thought and feeling might be restored.

* * *

In considering our whole relationship with Nature we might start with R. G. Collingwood's thoughts on the subject, as expressed in his book, *The Idea of Nature*, in which he identifies three distinct periods in European thought: the Classical, the Post-Renaissance, and the Modern. In each of these periods, man's vision of the Universe or Cosmos has changed radically.

In the first of these periods – the Classical, extending from the time of Ancient Greece (Fourth Century B. C.) to the middle of the Sixteenth Century – Nature was regarded as a living organism, permeated by mind.

In the next period – the Post-Renaissance, extending from the middle of the Sixteenth Century and into the Eighteenth Century – Nature is no longer regarded as an organism, possessed of intelligence and life and through the work of Galileo and Newton et al it becomes instead a "machine". No longer animate, Nature is now obedient to laws established from *"without"* by a Divine Creator.

In the third period of cosmological thought – extending from the late Eighteenth Century to the present day – Nature is no longer regarded as animate or mechanical. Through advances made principally in the fields of biochemistry, theoretical physics and historical study, the world of Nature is now identified with progressive change and development. Nature, like History, is characterised by the constant emergence of new things.

Each of these pictures of the Universe gives rise to distinctive figures of speech. The Ancient Greek view of Nature, which persisted down to the middle of the Sixteenth Century, lent itself to metaphor. As we have seen, the world was not simply "like" an animal; it was "animate". There was an intimate connection between man's body and the body of the world, between man's soul and the soul of the Universe.

In contrast, the early modern view of Nature is founded on "simile" and "likens" the natural world to a machine. In the same way, the modern view of Nature "likens" the processes observed by scientists in Nature to those observed by historians in human affairs.

According to this modern view, nothing is repeated in the world of Nature and progress is no longer cyclical but "progressive".

Though this may appear to be a cyclical process, Collingwood pointed out, in 1945, that what appears to be rotary or circular movement "is, in fact, a spiral movement in which the radius is constantly changing or the centre constantly displaced, or both." (Collingwood op. cit. 14) Remarkably, this analogy is reflected in the landmark discovery in 1953, by Crick and Watson, of the chemistry and structure of the DNA molecule which governs and determines human life. This structure turns out to be a Double Helix – a right-handed "spiral staircase", in which each tread is of the same size, at the same distance from the next, and turns at the same rate (J. Bronowski *The Ascent of Man* 253)

In this way, the broken circle of Donne's Universe is transformed into an evolutionary spiral of progress and, along with particle physics'"dance of energy", metaphor once again becomes reality: something which both Donne and Aristotle, ever the biologist, might have found reassuring.

* * *

Another way towards the unification of thought and feeling might be found in challenging the assumption that Bacon's thought is necessarily utilitarian, and focussing instead on the ethical dimension to his work.

Certainly, William Rawley, his personal secretary and chaplain, paints a very sympathetic portrait of him, far from the heartless go-getter that we sometimes assume him to have been. As a judge, Rawley tells us, Bacon was always tender-hearted, "looking upon the examples with the eye of severity, but upon the person with the eye of pity and compassion." At the same time, we are told, "he was free from malice" and "no revenger of injuries."

More to the point is Bacon's declaration in his Preface to his Instauratio Magna (1620) that the pursuit of knowledge must always be tempered by Charity:

"I humbly pray...that Knowledge being now discharged of that venom which the serpent infused into it, and which makes the mind of man to swell, we may not be wise above measure and sobriety, but cultivate truth in Charity...I would address one general admonition to all:

that they consider what are the true ends of Knowledge and that they seek it not either for pleasure of the mind, or for superiority to others; or for profit, or power, or any of these inferior things; but for the benefit and use of life; and that they perfect and govern it in Charity. For it was from lust of power that the angels fell, from lust of knowledge that man fell; but of Charity there can be no excess, neither did angel or man ever come in danger by it."

We are clearly a long way here from the narrow utilitarianism of Jeremy Bentham which saw legislation as "a matter of arithmetic" (*Theory of Legislation Cap* 8). Bacon's oft-repeated aim, to improve the human condition by means of philosophy and science, clearly derives not from a narrow utilitarian desire for profit and the advancement of special interests; but from a genuine concern for the creation of a better world for mankind through a true understanding of Nature.

Such an approach today would surely see Governments everywhere moving away from the "mathematics" of care and leaving behind the utilitarian calculus of pleasure and pain in addressing the needs of society. Pleasure for the many should not be sought at the expense of the few.

* * *

Nowhere is the need to reverse the utilitarian trajectory of modern science and technology more obvious than in our relationship with the natural world. The threat posed to planet Earth by the relentless march of material progress is clearly reflected in Climate change and the decline of bio-diversity.

Both these factors are the consequence of over-population, leading to over-consumption and over-production, resulting in the destruction of insect habitat through the process of deforestation and the out-pouring of carbon emissions. Addressing the issue of over-consumption clearly requires a moral revolution on the part of humans everywhere to bring about a change in our attitude towards each other and our environment. But how are we to be persuaded to accept such a change?

Governments, of course, can play a major role in this process but perhaps we all need to embrace a philosophy which unifies thought and feeling in addressing our planet's needs. One such philosophy is to be found in Gaia Theory.

Named after the Ancient Greek Goddess of Earth, the Gaia Theory is most closely associated with the work of the scientist and inventor, James Lovelock, and it first surfaced in his book, *Gaia – A New Look at Planet Earth*, which was published in 1979.

The Gaia Theory suggests that the entire world is a single living organism; that life has evolved so that it maintains Earth's stability and health; and that all forms of life incessantly modify the physical and chemical environment to their mutual advantage.

Although dismissed by many scientists as being little more than a fairy story about a Greek Goddess, the Gaia Theory does, in fact, have a background in science and observation. It is a theory derived from seeing Earth from the point of view of space and using arguments from thermodynamics.

It is very much the product of Lovelock's work on the Mars Viking Project during the 1960's, part of which involved establishing the viability of life on Mars. This revealed a dead atmosphere consisting of 95% Carbon Dioxide and 2.7% Nitrogen – a mixture incapable of sustaining life on the planet's surface. The contrast with Earth was striking. Looked at from the top down, from space, Earth's atmosphere revealed a strange mixture of unstable, almost combustible gases (78% Nitrogen, 21% Oxygen and only 0.3% Carbon Dioxide), which somehow always keep constant in composition. Why should such an improbable mixture of gases exist?

Lovelock's conclusion from this observation was that, for the atmosphere to keep constant, something must be regulating it and that somehow life at the surface of Earth was involved, in a process in which microbes, plants and animals combined actively to use the energy from sunlight to create an atmosphere suitable to sustain life.

Much of this part of his Gaia Theory is influenced by Lovelock's interpretation of Thermodynamics and the role of Entropy in Nature.

Entropy is a function of the Second Law of Thermodynamics, which states that heat passes only from hot bodies to cold and never the other way round. It may be defined as a quantity which measures the irreversible progress of heat in only one direction. It is a measurable and calculable quantity that increases or remains the same but never decreases. It is also the quantative measure of the relative disorder of a system.

Initially, at the beginning of the Universe, this Entropy in the world of Nature was very low but it has been growing ever since and the result, says Lovelock, is that natural processes always move towards an increase of disorder.

The natural tendency of the Universe, therefore, is to run down, to burn out; but, according to Lovelock, "far from being something tragic or a cause of sorrow, this universal tendency to decay benefits us...since without the decay of the Universe there could have been no Sun, whose super-abundant consumption of its stored energy is the source of our life." (Lovelock *The Ages of Gaia* 22)

Lovelock also points out that in Entropy Theory Boltzmann's Constant, expressed in the equation

$S=K\log W$, establishes that the less probable something is, the lower is its entropy. For Lovelock the most improbable thing of all is Life itself. It must, therefore, be associated with the lowest entropy and on this depends its capacity to avoid the universal tendency towards decay.

Gaia Theory, therefore, sees life on Earth as a system of mutual co-operation that is able to regulate the temperature and the composition of the Earth's surface and keep it comfortable for living organisms. According to this view natural selection favours organisms that actually improve their environment and this, of course, includes the human species. As Lovelock observes, "The Gaia Hypothesis implies that the stable state of our planet includes man as a part of, or a partner in a very democratic entity." (*Gaia – A new look at life on Planet Earth* 137)

This obviously poses a challenge to Darwinian Evolutionary Theory in which organisms adapt to environments and compete for their independent survival, which depends upon survival of the fittest. In a time of Climate change and declining bio-diversity, however, Gaia Theory may offer some hope for the future by emphasising the need for mankind to co-operate with the environment rather than to try to dominate it. Ultimately, our survival and that of every other life form depends upon low entropy and a change in our approach to the world of Nature. Bacon would surely have approved of such a strategy.

"If we see the world as a living organism," says Lovelock, "of which we are a part – not the owner, nor the tenant; not even a passenger – we could have a long time ahead of us and our species might survive for its allotted span. It is up to us to act personally in a way that is constructive." (*The Ages of Gaia* 236)

* * *

Education is another area in which thought and feeling might be reunited and this springs from the fact that the Scientific Revolution of the Seventeenth Century has had profound effects upon formal schooling. The world picture conceived by Aristotelian Cosmology had provided an explanation of physical reality which was satisfying to scholar and layman alike. As a result, tensions between "high" culture derived from formal education and "popular" culture derived from simply living in society were never really noticeable.

The Scientific Revolution of the Seventeenth Century, however, effectively destroyed this cultural harmony by divorcing the worlds of sense and intellect, of thought and feeling and creating in their stead an "aristocracy of intellect" (G. N. Clark) in which both scientist and poet create their own private worlds.

The "dissociation of sensibility" resulting from this separation of thought and feeling was, of course, initially confined to poets but its effects have since spread much further.

This is largely a consequence of the development of popular education since the Nineteenth Century, modelled on a diluted version of liberal education derived from Ancient Greece. This process, by identifying education with a culture that is no longer part of an organic whole and which has little connection with the everyday reality of people's lives, has created what is, in effect, a "museum culture." (See D. Conduct *Essays on a Liberal Education*)

This is clearly reflected in the Clarendon Report of 1864 whose discussion of the value of Greek and Latin in public school education, supplies what may still be considered to be a valid justification for much of what passes for academic study in our schools today: "As literature they (Greek and Latin) supply the most graceful and some of the noblest poetry, the finest elegance, the deepest philosophy, the wisest historical writing; and these excellences are such as to be appreciated keenly by young minds and to leave, as in fact they do, a lasting impression...the whole civilisation of modern Europe is really built upon the foundations laid two thousand years ago by two highly civilised nations on the shores of the Mediterranean..."

Of course, the prestige of this Classical tradition has waned considerably during the intervening years but if our educational practise has outgrown its dependence on the classics it is still very much influenced by the same concern for rational understanding and all-round moral and intellectual excellence so dear to the Ancient Greeks and Romans.

It is still possible to speak of children as "barbarians outside the gates" (R. S. Peters) and to conceive of education as the process whereby they are brought inside the citadel of civilisation, "so that they will understand and love what they see when they get there." In this way the rearing of children has come to be associated with the study and teaching of a narrow range of academic subjects which are supposed to develop mind and character and provide the necessary introduction to what is termed our "culture." But do they?

What we would seem to need is a culture and an education which respects the diversity and autonomy of human intelligence. Education is not some utilitarian tool to serve what are claimed to be the needs of society. We are all so much better than our ordinary lives allow us to be (J. B. Priestley) and in this sense education is not for life; life is for education and the State only exists to make this life possible.

* * *

We might conclude this discussion of how to re-unite thought and feeling by re-assessing the functions of the brain's right and left hemispheres.

That the brain is divided into left and right hemispheres, each in charge of their opposite side of the body, had been known for some time but that they functioned differently is largely the product of research by neuro-psychologists, such as Roger Sperry in the 1960's; research which came to associate the two hemispheres with quite distinctive activities: the left with speech, reading, writing and calculation, logic and analysis; the right with creativity, intuition and non-verbal communication through the arts.

Such research has led some social anthropologists to identify the left brain as the source of the logo-centric, materialistic dominance so characteristic of Western society – an outcome, we might add, of which Bacon would have heartily approved. Our working lives today sadly reflect this dominance.

Recent research (2013), however, has shown that neither hemisphere is dominant and that, in fact, they collaborate, providing in-put and support to both the brain's logical and creative activities. This gives support to the view that for a healthy outcome a balance needs to be struck between these two activities, with perhaps more emphasis being given to the creative side.

In pursuit of this goal, it has been suggested that a life style incorporating aerobic exercise, a healthy diet, fun and relaxation, the acquisition of new skills, a good night's sleep and the practise of daily meditation to combat cognitive decline in old age are all we really need to keep *both* hemispheres of our brain functioning properly.

Thought and feeling might truly then be one.

E. A. BURTT'S EVALUATION

In his essay on Bacon and the Dissociation of Sensibility, L. C. Knights references the work of E. A. Burtt on *The Metaphysical Foundations of Modern Science*. Published in 1924, Knights describes it as the best analysis for the non-scientific reader of the assumptions of Seventeenth Century science. After nearly one hundred years it still contains some interesting observations on the development of scientific thought in the Sixteenth and the Seventeenth Century, and the consequences there of.

In his work, Burtt contrasts the medieval world view, which saw man as the centre of the Universe and Nature as being both subordinate to him and fully intelligible to him, with the modern view, expressed by Bertrand Russell among others, which sees man as but a chance and temporary product of a blind, purposeless Nature and Earth as a speck in space. (E. A. Burtt *The Metaphysical foundations of Modern Science* 23-4)

Modern philosophy, since Berkley, Hume and Kant, Burtt claims, has been an unsuccessful attempt to challenge Russell's view and to re-instate the medieval view of man's importance in the cosmic scheme of things.

Significantly, in trying to explain why this attempt has failed, Burtt makes no reference to Eliot's "dissociation of sensibility" (1921), which is clearly one of the major consequences of our changed view of the Universe. Instead, he prefers to focus on the scientific work associated with Descartes and Newton, rather than on changes taking place in the world of poetry.

Before doing so, however, Burtt makes the point that the failure of modern philosophy to counter Russell's view of the Universe could simply be because this view 'is' true. The failure may also spring from the fact that the terminology of modern philosophy, with its emphasis upon force, mass, space and time, as opposed to causality, essence and substance, has become scientific. As a result, in the words of Max Born, "theoretical physics is now actually philosophy."

Burtt's approach therefore is to pursue what he describes as "a neglected type of historical inquiry" into the philosophy of early modern science. (Burtt op. cit. 29)

In the course of this inquiry he identifies Descartes (1596-1650) as a major force behind the emergence of a new view of the Universe and man's place in it. This is very much the consequence of Descartes' faith in the power of maths (Analytical Geometry) as a key to understanding the Universe and his use of the Method of Universal Doubt to undermine the world of sense observation.

In this way, Descartes makes a mathematical structure of the material world, independent of man but intelligible to him, while atoning for removing man from this structure by his theory of metaphysical dualism, separating mind from body.

Descartes' dualism posits the existence of two quite separate worlds of "res extensa" and "res cogitans". The former is a geometrical world whose essence is 'extension' and is only knowable through pure mathematics. This spatial world, which extends infinitely throughout all Space, becomes a vast machine, quite independent of human thought or attention. (Burtt op. cit. 118)

The latter, "res cogitans", is the inner world of the mind, localised and wholly confined within the body – a world of secondary qualities such as will, perception, feeling and imagining. This universe of the mind, claims Burtt, "comes to be pictured as locked up behind the confused and deceitful media of the senses, away from the independent, extended realm, the universe of matter, in a petty and insignificant series of locations inside of human bodies." (Burtt op. cit. 123)

This dualism is the true source of our dissociation of sensibility and according to Burtt it has brought about "an incalculable change in the view point of the world held by intelligent opinion in Europe." (Burtt op. cit. 124)

Descartes' metaphysics was, of course, reinforced by the work of Newton (1643-1727) and Burtt devotes a lot of space to assessing his pivotal role in shaping the Scientific Revolution of the Seventeenth Century. Newton's union of maths and experimental method enabled him to identify a mechanical universe, governed by universal laws and quite outside of man's control. In this way, he gave his authority to a new view of the Cosmos which saw in man a puny, irrelevant spectator of a vast mathematical system whose regular motions according to mechanical principles now constituted the world of Nature.

Like L. C. Knights, Burtt is critical of some aspects of the scientific revolution which took place in the Seventeenth Century and he describes the cultural consequences of Newtonian mechanics and Cartesian dualism in the following terms:

"The glorious romantic universe of Dante and Milton, that set no bounds to the imagination of man as it played over space and time, had now been swept away. Space was identified with the realm of geometry, time with the continuity of number. The world that people had thought themselves living in – a world rich with colour and sound, redolent with fragrances, filled with gladness, love and beauty, speaking everywhere of purposive harmony and creative ideals – was crowded now into minute corners in the brains of scattered organic beings. The really important world outside was a world hard, cold, colourless, silent and dead; a world of quantity, a world of mathematically computable motions in mechanical regularity... In Newton the Cartesian metaphysics...finally overthrew Aristotelianism and became the predominant world-view of modern times." (Burtt op. cit. 238-9)

In this way, the Aristotelian picture of Nature which had seen it as a sociable and human world, made to serve man's needs and form a companion to his reason was transformed into a monotonous mathematical machine in which the very substance of the physical world, the things that made it alive and lovely and spiritual were cast aside, confined to a small corner of our nervous system. The world had become a mathematical machine and mankind "devotees of mathematical science." (Burtt op. cit. 297)

There are clearly echoes here of L. C. Knights'concern about the "spiritual impoverishment" arising from the Scientific Revolution of the Seventeenth Century; but where Knights sees a solution to the problem through a union of Reason and Sensibility, Burtt sees the way forward through a reassertion of the role of mind in the pursuit of knowledge and understanding. As he observes of the progress of science in the Seventeenth Century:

"It was of the utmost importance for this whole subsequent development of science and philosophy that the place reluctantly admitted to the mind was pitifully meagre, never exceeding a varying portion of the body with which it is allied." (Burtt op. cit. 122)

Burtt, therefore, calls for a new metaphysic and a new cosmology to be reached by "extensive historical analysis" and the exercise of mind: "The whole vast realm which science reveals finds its rational order and meaning in the knowing activity of the mind. So far from being a curious sensitive substance present in a small corner of the brain, or even an activity of the nervous system, mind seems to be a unique activity... An adequate cosmology will only begin to be written when an adequate philosophy of mind has appeared... Mind has the power to feel, to idealise, to create its world into something significantly better, as well as to know it." (Burtt op. cit. 323-4)

For Burtt, writing in 1924 therefore, mathematics was clearly not the only key to reality and Heisenberg's Uncertainty Principle (1927) and Godel's Incompleteness Theorem (1931) did much to substantiate his claim that there is more to the Universe than meets the mathematical eye.

MIND OVER MATTER

*Metaphor

*Benevolence

*Native American Wisdom

Metaphor and Truth

The conscious rejection of metaphor as anything more than a pretty ornament is a distinguishing feature of the dissociation of sensibility. One way of restoring some unity to our thought and feeling, therefore, might be to enrich our language by the more frequent use of metaphor. A few examples:

*Life is a book.

*People are places, places where the mind lives.

*God is the quantum of love.

*The human race is a family, not a competition.

*We are forged by many hands and are all threads of something or someone else.

*Believe in the holy contour of life.

*Memory is a Swiss Cheese, full of holes which are portals into time.

* The Universe has its origin in a 'sea' of energy and an 'ocean' of love.

Benevolence

In response to Bacon's plea for a union of Charity and Knowledge in human affairs, we might consider exploring the African philosophy of Ubuntu, in which a person becomes a person through other people.

This philosophy represents a serious challenge to the Eighteenth Century Enlightenment obsession with Reason, which arises out of Descartes' "I think; therefore I am." Ubuntu humanism, in contrast, identifies existence with the act of sharing and the belief in mutual personhood: "I share; therefore I am."

According to this philosophy, a person is a social being whose fulfilment depends upon kindness to others.

Native American Wisdom

Our general responsibility for the care of Nature's resources and the whole community is a theme very dear to the Native American tribes of North America and the following extracts draw attention to the importance of that role. They have in them some echoes of Lovelock's Gaia Theory and we can learn much from them.

"Hear me, four quarters of the world –
a relative am I! Give me the strength
to walk the soft earth, a relative to all that is."
Black Elk (1863-1950) Sioux Holy Man

"Out of the Indian approach to life there came a great freedom – an intense and absorbing love for Nature; a respect for life; an enriching faith in a Supreme Power; and principles of truth, honesty, generosity and brotherhood... I venture to think that the man who sat in his tipi, meditating on life and its meaning, accepting the kinship of all creatures, and acknowledging his unity with the universe of things was infusing into his being the true essence of civilisation."

Luther Standing Bear (1868-1939) Sioux Chief.

Source: "Native American Wisdom" Running Press Philadelphia

POSTSCRIPT

TOWARDS

A UNION OF SCIENCE AND RELIGION

- *MYTHOS AND LOGOS* -

Another way to re-unite thought and feeling and to repair the dissociation of sensibility might be to reconsider the role of science and religion in our lives.

In her study of religious fundamentalism in her book, *The Battle for God*, Karen Armstrong attempts to do this by drawing attention to the role of *mythos and logos* in shaping our beliefs. She sees religious fundamentalism, whether American, Jewish or Islamic, as a response to the challenge posed by the Scientific Revolution of the Seventeenth Century which has taken Western society and the rest of the world in a quite different direction from that pursued in the past: a world dominated by technology and the notion of progressive change. The effect of this development has been to separate two ways of thinking and acquiring knowledge, which scholars have called *mythos* and *logos*.

Karen Armstrong makes the point that before the Eighteenth Century these two ways of thinking could be said to have worked in harmony with each other. "The *mythos* of a society provided people with a context that made sense of their day-to-day lives; it directed their attention to the eternal and the universal... *Logos* was equally important...the rational, pragmatic and scientific thought that enabled men and women to function well in the world." (*The Battle for God* xiii – xiv)

For a long time this harmony was reflected, as we have seen, in the peaceful co-existence of Christianity alongside Aristotelian cosmology.

This harmony was effectively destroyed by the Scientific Revolution of the Seventeenth Century and the Eighteenth Century Enlightenment which followed. With advances in science and technology, together with Bacon's crusade on behalf of the utilitarian ethic, many people in Europe and America began to think that *Logos* was the only means to truth and to regard *Mythos*, typically in the form of Religion, as false and superstitious.

Religious fundamentalism is essentially an attempt to challenge this perception and to reassert the role of *Mythos* in our lives; but, as Karen Armstrong points out, its effect has been to turn faith into a new kind of *Logos*. We need, therefore, to recognise and accept the respective limits of both *Mythos* and *Logos* if we are to establish a more harmonious relationship between Science and Religion.

We might start with Religion, which has its origin in myth, in particular the myths of Creation. The fundamental function of such myths is to provide mankind with an explanation which might give some meaning to life. In time, such myths, which cannot be demonstrated by rational proof, have become transformed into a reality by the development of rituals and ceremonies designed to foster and encourage belief in them. In the process, *mythos* has come to assume much of the character of *logos*, and religion has become inseparable from doctrines and practises which claim to give meaning to our lives and give us access to the divine.

As a result, organised religion, virtually everywhere, has become a kind of dogmatic alternative to *logos*. This process actually hinders our spiritual growth and creates an unnecessary gulf between science and religion.

A simpler religious path, leading to a more authentic *mythos*, might be found through mysticism, such as that of Dame Julian of Norwich in her *Revelations of Divine Love*. These *Revelations* reveal to us a God who is not some Old Testament super-power or New Testament missionary telling us how to live our lives; but a servant-king and displaced God: a man of sorrows and acquainted with grief. As the Anglican theologian, Austin Farrer once observed, "God did not send us an explanation; he sent us his son."

Dame Julian certainly does not see God in terms of rules and rituals, but as Love, the source of all Creation. Unfortunately, this is a flawed Creation since the love behind it is freely given and must be freely received. God's love cannot be forced upon us and we are all free to accept or reject it. This freedom of choice is what lies behind our broken universe and our dysfunctional world.

In an attempt to repair this situation, I believe that God re-entered his Creation in the person of his son, Jesus Christ, and became man. This re-entry occurred in an historical time and place, against the background of a Jewish religion, dating back to 1000 B.C. and located in the Middle East.

Certain features of the Jewish faith help to explain why God chose the Jews to provide the setting for this inauguration of a new Creation.

From the outset, the Jews identified themselves as the people of Yahweh and their commitment to a single, national God set them apart from other religions. This is made abundantly clear in *Deuteronomy*, one of the earliest books of the Old Testament, in which the Jews are told: "You have recognised the Lord as your God; you are to conform to his ways… The Lord has recognised you this day as His Special Possession." *Deuteronomy* 26, 17-18.

The Jews identified this God as the source of all Creation but recognised that His Creation was marred by human sin and rebellion. They believed, however, that the goal of history was a new Creation through which God's original intention would be fulfilled.

They further believed that God would, at some point in time, intervene in history by sending a saviour, or Messiah, to deliver them from suffering and injustice. In this way the Jewish faith came to provide the necessary framework for God's re-entry into Creation. Without it, Christianity would not have been possible.

Christ, a Jew, is a product and expression of these Jewish beliefs and he clearly saw himself as the fulfilment of the Old Law of Moses, the Prophets, and the Psalms, (Luke 24 • 44). In fulfilment of these beliefs, however, the role he assumes is not that of some Master of the Universe but that of a Just Man, bearing the sins of others and going meekly to his death for them. (*Isaiah* 53)

In this way, Christ's birth and death establish an entirely new relationship between God and Man: one built not upon dominance, control and blind obedience but on the unconditional giving and receiving of love – a new relationship, foretold in the *Prophecy of Jeremiah*, (31.31 – 34), and one written not on tablets of stone but in our hearts.

Seen in these terms, the love which fills the Universe is extremely vulnerable: an infinitely small, "infinitely gentle, infinitely suffering thing." And nowhere is this vulnerability more poignantly expressed than in the human form of Jesus Christ, through whom God, for a brief moment in time, re-enters His Creation, not to rule and control us, but to remind us of the importance of love in our lives. We have no need of a religion built on the supposed authority of rituals and regulations. Love is all we need.

This is Dame Julian's vision of the Divine and it provides us with some explanation of the "why?" of Creation; but to understand its "how?" requires us to embrace Science.

Modern theories of Science, like all Creation myths, attempt to explain how the Universe originated and why its existence and structure are the way they are. Stephen Hawking, and many others, identify its beginning with the finite moment of the Big Bang, when all matter was squashed into zero size. This theory owes much to the discovery in the 1920's that the Universe is in a state of overall expansion, which implies a finite origin; and this has been further reinforced by the discovery of cosmic background radiation in the mid – 1960's.

The commonly accepted model of the Universe, therefore, suggests that it began in an infinitely compact and singular state, enclosing a space even smaller than an atomic particle. The beginning of the Universe occurred when this compact ball grew, not in a violent explosion, but through rapid expansion in micro-seconds which saw the creation of the four basic physical forces of gravity, electro-magnetism, strong nuclear and weak inter-action. Together, these four forces shape the Universe.

Clearly such a model of the Universe leaves room for some consideration of the role of Super Nature in Creation (see 1950-Papal Encyclical of Pope Pius XII); and it is perhaps no coincidence that the Big Bang theory has its theoretical origins in the work of Abbé Georges Lemaitre, a Clerical physicist at Louvain University. Published in the 1930's, Lemaitre's theory of creation postulated the explosion of a single, primordial atom – "Lemaitre's Egg", as it has been called – and modern science in the Twenty-first Century still gives some support to this theory.

Moving from the infinitely large world of astronomical observation, we can turn to the infinitely small world of particle physics and quantum mechanics and, remarkably, we may find that this also leaves room for some supernatural explanation of Creation. In the world of the infinitely small, "we are immediately struck by the chaotic dance of the elementary components of matter which fluctuate, oscillate and change nature at a frenetic pace… At a microscopic level, matter relentlessly follows the laws of quantum mechanics, dominated by chance and the principle of uncertainty. Nothing stays still. Everything seethes in an extra-ordinary, constantly changing variety of states and possibilities." (Guido Tonelli *Genesis* 17)

Amazingly, quantum mechanics and particle physics have established that in this microscopic world photons and electrons, the smallest particles in the material world, can be in many places at the same time. Their weirdness supplies a key to understanding the initial stages of the Big Bang and the inflationary expansion which followed.

The Large Hadron Collider at Cern exists to further this research and in 2012 the discovery of the Higgs-Boson particle gave rise to speculation that Science was getting closer to identifying the "God" particle responsible for the creation of the Universe. The Higgs-Boson discovery, however, has not provided a conclusive answer to such questions and in 2022 the search for the "Fifth Force" continues.

At this point Science, the supreme expression of *Logos*, might well reach out to *Mythos* for some help in understanding such complexity and the Taoist philosophy of the Chinese mystic, Lao-Tzu who lived 2500 years ago, might be of some assistance. He identifies the primal cause of Creation in the following terms:

"There is a thing inherent and natural

*Which existed before heaven and earth,
Motionless and fathomless,
It stands alone and never changes.
It pervades everything and is illimitable.
It may be regarded as the source of the Universe,
I do not know what it is...
I call it Tao and name it as Supreme...
From the Tao the infinite complexity of the Cosmos
Has taken shape."*

(From Lao-Tzu *Tao-Te-Ching*, quoted by Philip Freund Myths of Creation 43)

There are echoes of this Taoist thought in Dame Julian's account of one of her own mystical experiences and it, too, may be of some help in bridging the gulf between Science and Religion:

"*He showed me a little thing, the size of a hazelnut, in the palm of my hand and it was as round as a ball. I looked at it with my mind's eye and I thought, 'What can this be?' And answer came: 'It is all that is made.' I marvelled that it could last, for I thought it might have crumbled to nothing, it was so small. And answer came into my mind: 'It lasts and ever shall because God loves it.' And all things have being through the love of God.*"

An echo of William Blake's "infinity in the palm of your hand", Julian's vision of a hazelnut enables us to see Love as a physical and creative force and God as the primordial atom, the Quantum of Love.

Like the Tao and the electron particle, Love is the One: infinitely small, in everyone, in everything, in every place, at every time. We know this partly through the study of quantum mechanics, but mainly through the exercise of love in our lives.

For both Dame Julian and Lao-Tzu, Love seeks a home in every heart but it cannot force its company on us. We have to welcome it in and we don't have to try and understand it. As another mystical source – the Fourteenth Century *Cloud of Unknowing* – tells us: *"It is enough to feel moved in love by something, though you know not what it is."*

Such a conclusion requires us to abandon the quest for certainty in our lives. As I have tried to point out in my discussion of religion, this means moving away from the blind acceptance of authority and the obsessive attachment to rules and rituals and embracing the mystery of God's unconditional love for us all. At the same time, however, it requires us to give up our search for any certainty in science where, in fact, the *challenge* to certainty is welcomed and where nothing is what it seems to be.

On the cosmic level our eyes register the light of dead stars and we see not the present but the past; while, at the level of the infinitely small – the electron particle – not even atomic events can be described with absolute certainty. Science, like Religion, therefore, should surrender its search for certainty and encourage in us a spirit of humanity and tolerance. If it does not, then the results can be damaging for the individual and disastrous for society in general.

This was the point made by the scientist, Jacob Bronowski, in his famous television series, "The Ascent of Man," when, standing outside the extermination camp of Auschwitz, in the marshy ground over which the ashes of cremated Jews were scattered, he stretched out his hands in the stagnant water and made the following plea for tolerance and understanding: "We have to cure ourselves of the itch for absolute knowledge and power... We have to touch people." (*The Ascent of Man* 241)

Love is all we need and to love our neighbour we do not have to know calculus or the Ten Commandments.

God *and* science meet in the infinite smallness of Creation, *et amor vincit omnia*.

Anthropomorphism

Anthropomorphism, the attribution of human characteristics to inhuman forms, has a long cultural history and some version of it might help us to re-unite thought and feeling and repair our relationship with the world of Nature.

In his essay, "Why look at Animals?",published in 1977,John Berger attempts to do this by pointing out that corporate capitalism in the twentieth century had effectively broken every tradition which had previously mediated between mankind and Nature. Before this rupture, animals in particular had been with man at the centre of his world and not simply as a source of food, work, transport or clothing. "Animals,"claims Berger, "first entered the imagination as messengers and promises... sometimes oracular, sometimes sacrificial."Animals were found in 8 out of 12 signs of the Zodiac and humanity's first symbols were of animal form as reflected in the Palaeolithic cave art of Lascaux.

Early on, then, mankind became anthropomorphic, delighting in attributing human characteristics to natural objects, especially animals and assigning human feelings to them. Berger quotes Aristotle as evidence of such anthropomorphism. "In a number of animals," writes Aristotle, "we observe gentleness and fierceness, mildness or cross- temper, courage or timidity and with regard to intelligence something akin to sagacity." In the same way, Robert Burton in his "Anatomy of Melancholy", quotes numerous examples of the love often displayed by animals for humans.

In the last two centuries, however, animals in this sense, Berger declares, have gradually disappeared and today we 'live' without them. The result is that everywhere animals 'disappear 'and become marginalised, leading Berger to conclude that "the look between animal and man which may have played a crucial role in the development of human society and with which all men had always lived until less than a century ago, has been extinguished".

Berger identifies Descartes' dualism as the source of this separation, for in dividing absolutely body from the soul, Descartes "bequeathed the body to the laws of physics and mechanics and, since animals were soulless, the animal was reduced to the model of a machine."

At the same time, this reduction of the animal to the level of a machine is part of the same process by which humans have been reduced to isolated, productive and consuming units. It is no coincidence, observes Berger, that "nearly all modern techniques of social conditioning were first established with animal experiments." As a result, the mechanical view of the animal's work capacity has come to be applied to that of workers in the form of the scientific management of industry.

Is it too fanciful to think that anthropomorphism, in the form of a more sympathetic approach to animal welfare, might help to restore a union of thought and feeling and create a more healthy balance between human society and the natural world?

www.ingramcontent.com/pod-product-compliance
Lightning Source LLC
Chambersburg PA
CBHW052208110526
44591CB00012B/2129